P9-CCR-487

THIS BOOK
BELONGS TO:

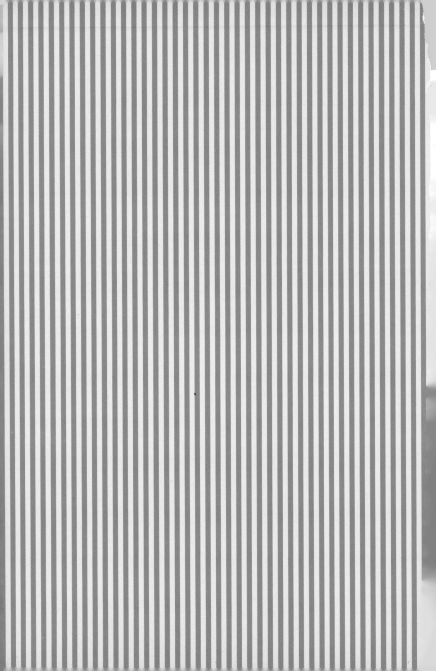

Unlikely Friendships

for Kids

Book Two

The Dog and the Piglet

and Four Other True Stories of Animal Friendships

by

JENNIFER S. HOLLAND

WORKMAN PUBLISHING
NEW YORK

For Cree, an awesome little dude

Library of Congress Cataloging-in-Publication Data is available.

ISBN: 978-0-7611-7012-9

Design by Raquel Jaramillo

Photo Credits: COVER: Front, BARCROFT/FAME; INTERIOR: p. 1, p.
10, p. 12, p. 13, p. 15, pp. 16-17, p. 19 BARCROFT/FAME; p. 4 Sebastien
Burel/Shutterstock; p. 6 Jennifer Hayes; p. 20, p. 22, pp. 24-25, p. 26
ZooWorld, Panama City Beach, FL; p. 28 © Rhino & Lion Nature Reserve;
p. 30 anyaivanova/Shutterstock; p. 34, p. 37 © Jeffery R. Werner/
IncredibleFeatures.com; p. 38, p. 43, p. 44 © Rina Deych.

Workman books are available at special discounts when purchased in
bulk for premiums and sales promotions as well as for fund-raising or
educational use. Special editions or book excerpts can also be created
to specification. For details, contact the Special Sales Director at the
address below or send an e-mail to specialsales@workman.com.

Workman Publishing Company, Inc.
225 Varick Street
New York, NY 10014-4381

www.workman.com

Printed in the United States of America
First printing April 2012

Contents

R eaders new to this series may want to know how I started writing about unlikely animal friendships. Here's the story.

A few years ago, I went scuba diving on Australia's Great Barrier Reef. This is a very special place in the ocean. Thousands of different types of fish live in or around the coral reef.

I noticed a puffer fish swimming near me. The puffer fish was about the size of a softball. He was alone. The puffer fish did not seem to be afraid of me. I swam with him for a little while. He did not swim away.

I went back to the same area the next day. The puffer fish was there. This time, he was not alone. He was swimming

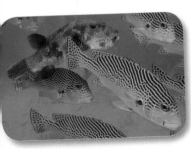

with a school of fish called sweetlips.

Sweetlips are very colorful fish. They have wide mouths, which is probably how they got their name. Sweetlips do not usually swim with puffer fish. But that is exactly what was happening. The sweetlips and the puffer fish were swimming together.

I went back again the next day. They were still together! What was going on? Why were they swimming together? I thought it was very interesting that two animals from different species would be hanging around each other like they were friends. It made me wonder if other animals became friends with animals that were very different from them.

I am a science writer. I write about animals. So I decided to write a book about animals of different species who had become friends. I had heard some of these stories before. The story of Owen and Mzee, a tortoise and a hippopotamus who became friends after surviving a tsunami, was already famous. But I went looking for stories I had never heard before. I talked with people all around the world. I looked at many photographs. Sometimes the animal friendships were so unlikely that I wondered if they were true. But when I checked them out, they were!

Five of those stories are in this book. I hope you enjoy reading them as much as I enjoyed writing them!

—Jennifer S. Holland

Chapter One

The Dog and the Piglet

Katjinga was a dog who lived on a farm in Germany. She was a Rhodesian ridgeback. This breed of dog is quite large. Many years ago, people in Africa used ridgebacks to help them hunt lions. These dogs were not only big, they were very fierce.

11

Katjinga was not a fierce hunting dog, though. She was a very gentle dog. And one night on the farm she proved just how gentle she was.

On that cold night,
a little potbellied pig was
born. The farmer found
the piglet all alone.

The piglet's mother was
nowhere in sight. Perhaps she
had gone to look for food. Or
perhaps she had abandoned
the tiny piglet. Sometimes
animals leave their babies
when they are so small that
they are not likely to survive.
This piglet was so tiny and
weak, he did not look like he
would live through the night.

The farmer decided to name the shivering piglet Paulinchen. Then he took him back to his home and placed him near Katjinga. He hoped Paulinchen would get warm by lying near the huge dog. And he hoped Katjinga would not mind a tiny potbellied piglet lying down next to her! Katjinga was a ridgeback, after all—and ridgebacks once hunted lions. Would this ridgeback be nice to the piglet?

Luckily, Katjinga was more
than nice to Paulinchen.
She started to mother the
little piglet! She nuzzled
him. She licked him all
over just like mama dogs
lick their puppies.

The next day, Katjinga and
Paulinchen were snuggled
up like two peas in a pod.

16

Katjinga didn't mind when the
piglet tried to nurse from her—
even though she had no milk!

In time, when Paulinchen was strong enough, the farmer reunited the piglet with his real mother. But Paulinchen never forgot Katjinga.
Every time he saw the big brown dog on the farm, he ran up to nuzzle her—just like Katjinga did to him on the night that he was born.

Chapter Two

The Orangutan and the Cat

Tonda, an old orangutan that lived in a zoo, was not known for being nice. In fact, she was downright grouchy—not just with the zookeepers, but even with her own mate! And yet, when her mate died, the zookeepers noticed that Tonda got very, very sad.

The zookeepers tried giving Tonda lots of toys to lift her spirits. They filled her days with activities. But Tonda was still sad. She started to eat less. Then the zookeepers had an idea. What if Tonda got introduced to a new friend?

And they had just the friend in mind: a tabby cat named T. K. For some reason, the cat wasn't afraid of the

grumpy old orangutan.
And the orangutan, who
was aways rough with other
animals, was very gentle
with T. K. The zookeepers
noticed that Tonda got
angry every time they took
T. K. away. But whenever
they let T. K. play with Tonda,
the orangutan became happy.
So they let T. K. stay with
Tonda all the time!

T. K. became very important
to Tonda. The orangutan
always kept her eye on him.

She would scoop up T. K. and carry him to her bed at night, then tuck him under a blanket to keep him warm. She played with him all the time, and often hugged him tenderly.

The cat loved Tonda, too. He
liked to lick Tonda and rub his
face against Tonda's.

The zookeepers believe
that T. K. saved Tonda's life.
After she became friends
with the cat, she started
eating again.

Tonda never changed her
ways with other animals.
She was still mean and
grumpy to the rest of the
world. But to the cat who
saved her life, the orangutan
was always as gentle as
a lamb.

Chapter Three

The Hippopotamus and the Goat

A hippopotamus is not a good house pet. Just ask the family who tried to raise a hippo named Humphrey!

To start with, hippos are the third-largest land animals in the world. Only elephants and rhinoceroses are bigger. But even though they grow to be huge, hippos don't start out that way. A baby hippo is only about the size of a large dog. A dog isn't too big to keep inside a house, so it didn't seem like a baby hippo would be too big, either.

At first, everything went very well for Humphrey. He liked to sit on the furniture. He enjoyed hanging out with people. But what he liked most was swimming in the backyard pool. Hippopotamuses usually live near rivers, where they spend much of their days in the water.

After about six months, Humphrey got too big to live in the house. The family tried to move him outside. But Humphrey was a little spoiled by then. He wanted to live in the house—not in the yard. So he broke down the door to get inside!

That may sound cute, but
Humphrey was no longer
the size of a dog. He was
the size of a small car! If
Humphrey cuddled on the
bed with the family, he
would break the bed!

The family moved Humphrey
to a nearby game reserve,
where he would be cared
for. At first Humphrey was
lonely. But he soon became
friends with another animal
on the game reserve—a
pygmy goat.

It was a strange pair: the giant hippo and the tiny goat. They became inseparable. Humphrey started copying the goat's behavior. He would try to climb the fences of his pen, just like the goat did. No one had ever seen a hippo trying to climb a fence before. Then again, no one had ever tried to keep a hippo inside a house before, either. Humphrey was a very special hippo—that's for sure!

Chapter Four

The Deer and the Dog

Dillie was a white-tailed deer that had been born blind. She was unable to eat or stand up on her bony little legs. Since she would not have survived in her natural environment, a veterinarian decided to bring the tiny deer home to live with her family.

This vet also took care of a lot of other animals, including a poodle named Lady.

Lady was a great comfort to Dillie. She let the frightened deer lie next to her on the couch. She licked her all over. Dillie started licking Lady in return.

The two became best friends. They played tug-of-war with stuffed animals. And they got into mischief together, too. Dillie sometimes grabbed food from high shelves for Lady to snack on!

Dillie and Lady even slept in the same bed, though Dillie sometimes kicked poor Lady onto the floor. Lady never seemed to mind, though. Good friends never do.

Chapter Five

The Iguana and the Cat

New York City is home to a lot of things: the Empire State Building, the Yankees, the Statue of Liberty, and Central Park. But one thing it is definitely not is a home for iguanas, which is why this story is strange in many ways.

One day, as a man was walking to work, he came across a small iguana on the street. Iguanas usually live in Central or South America. What was an iguana doing on a New York City street? No one knows.

But the man did know that a small iguana would not survive on the streets of New York. He brought the iguana to a friend who often took in stray animals. His friend welcomed the little iguana

and named him Sobe. In time,
the small iguana grew to be
four-and-a-half-feet long!

A short while after giving
Sobe a home, the same
woman found a stray cat
near her house. He was
very sick. He had pneumonia
and an eye infection, and
he was covered with fleas.
So the woman took the
cat home and nursed him
back to health. She named
him Johann.

The first time Johann
met Sobe, the iguana
hissed. He puffed himself
up to make himself look
big. This is what iguanas
do in the wild to scare
away predators. But the
cat wasn't scared at all.
He just rubbed up against
the iguana's rough skin
and purred. Sobe calmed
down. He closed his
eyes and let the cat rub
against his face.

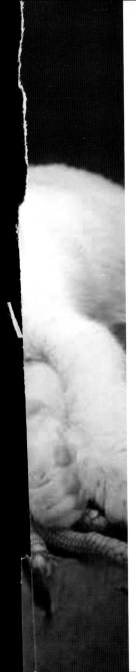

After that, the two
were always together.
Johann would clean
Sobe, and Sobe would
follow Johann all around
the house. Sobe would
climb onto the bed to
sleep with Johann. The
two were often found
curled up next to each
other: Johann with his
head leaning on Sobe's
body, and Sobe with his
mouth turned up in
what looked very much
like a smile.

Animal List

 cat: Common house pet that is also an excellent hunter. Cats have been friends with humans for thousands of years.

 dog: Common house pet related to the gray wolf. Dogs have been friends with humans for thousands of years.

 elephant: Large mammal with big ears, a long trunk, and two ivory tusks. Elephants live in Africa and Asia, and are the largest living land animals.

 goat: Mammal with hollow horns that curve backward. Goats are related to sheep, but they usually have straight hair.

 hippopotamus: Large mammal that lives in Africa and spends most of the time in the water. Its name means "river horse."

 iguana: Large lizard with scales along its back and loose skin hanging from its neck. It eats plants and lives in the tropics.

 lion: Big cat that lives mostly in Africa. Lions are the only big cats that live in groups, which are called *prides*.

 orangutan: Large ape with reddish-brown hair and long arms. Orangutans live in trees and eat mostly plants.

 piglet: A baby pig.

poodle: Active, intelligent dog with a curly coat. It can be small, medium-size, or large, and makes a good house pet.

 potbellied pig: Small pig with a round belly and straight tail. Potbellied pigs come from Asia and have either black, white, or black-and-white coats.

 puffer fish: Fish that can puff itself up into a ball and has lots of spines to keep predators away. It is also called *blowfish*.

 pygmy goat: Small goat that eats mostly greens and grains. The word *pygmy* means "a person or thing very small for its kind."

 rhinoceros: Large, plant-eating mammal from Africa and Asia that has thick skin and one or two heavy horns on its snout.

 Rhodesian ridgeback: Large dog from Africa that was once used to hunt lions. It is known for being fierce and very brave.

 sweetlips: Fish with large lips that often lives in coral reefs. Sweetlips are usually found alone or in small groups.

 tortoise: Reptile that lives on land and is protected by a hard shell. It is closely related to the turtle.

 white-tailed deer: Medium-size mammals that live in North America. Males have antlers and females do not.

Word and Phrase List

abandoned: Left behind.
behavior: The way an animal or person usually acts.
breed: Type of animal, especially a dog or cat.
coral reef: A chain of underwater coral and limestone rocks near the surface of the ocean where fish and other sea creatures live.
fierce: Unfriendly and aggressive.
game reserve: An area of land where animals live and are visited by tourists.
inseparable: Always together.
mate: An animal's partner.
mother: To take care of a baby.
natural environment: The area in the wild where an animal is best able to live.
nurse: To drink milk from a mother's breast. It can also mean to help someone who is sick to get well.
pneumonia: A sickness of the lungs that makes it hard to breathe.
predator: An animal that hunts and eats other animals.
reunited: Brought together again.
scuba dive: To swim underwater using an oxygen tank and mask to breathe.
species: A group of animals of the same kind.
stray cat: A cat that has no home or owner.
tabby cat: A house cat with a striped and spotted coat.
tsunami: A big sea wave, caused by an earthquake or a volcanic eruption under the sea, that often leads to a flood.
veterinarian: An animal doctor, sometimes called a *vet* for short.
zookeeper: A person who takes care of animals in a zoo.

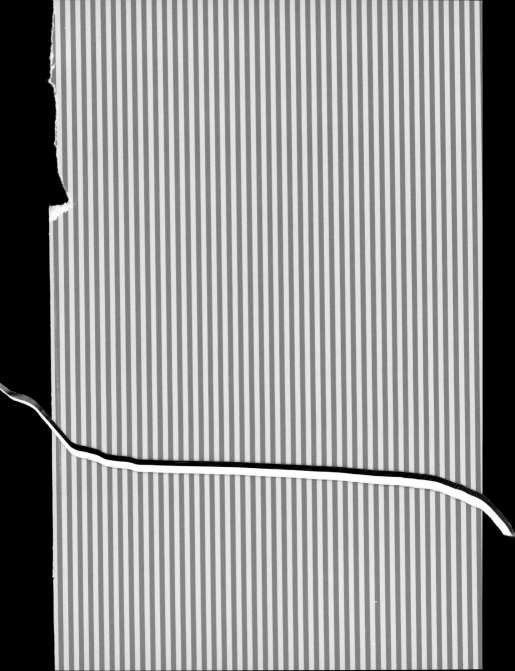